Dedication

For the parents who love fiercely, advocate tirelessly, and believe endlessly—

Your strength, patience, and compassion light the way for your extraordinary children.

This is for you and for them—a celebration of every small victory, every big feeling, and every unique, beautiful moment in between.

Author's Note

My name is Molly. I have Autism and ADHD. With my Mum's help, I wrote this book to help other children like me with daily challenges, especially those related to sensory sensitivities and struggling with completing daily boring tasks.

For World Book Day I was uncomfortable in fancy dress, so if I wrote my own book so I could wear what I wanted and be myself. I hope you enjoy the story and that it helps you manage the things that bother you.

Molly's Helpful Checklist

Helping Kids with ADHD Build Confidence, Focus, and Routines

By Molly Heald and Kate Heald

Molly's Helpful Checklist:

Tackling Tricky Tasks Together

Molly is a bright and imaginative 8-year-old who loves to explore and create.
She has a vivid imagination and enjoys painting colorful pictures of her adventures.
However, some everyday tasks feel a bit tricky for Molly.

One morning, as Molly was getting dressed for school, she shouted, 'I hate socks!' They felt scratchy and uncomfortable. She tried pulling them up, folding them down, and turning them inside out, but nothing seemed to help. Frustrated, Molly decided to talk to her teacher, Mrs. Sherriff, about it.

At school, Molly approached Mrs. Sherriff. "Mrs. Sherriff, my socks feel really scratchy, and I don't like wearing them," she said.

Mrs. Sherriff smiled kindly. "I understand, Molly. Sometimes, certain fabrics can feel uncomfortable on our skin. Let's try finding socks made from materials like cotton or bamboo, which might feel softer on your skin. We can also look for seamless socks to avoid irritation, or maybe you don't wear any at all."

Molly nodded, feeling hopeful. That evening, Molly and her Mum went shopping and found some soft, seamless cotton socks.

The next day, Molly wore them to school and felt much better.

A few days later, Molly faced another challenge. She didn't enjoy brushing her teeth. The taste of the toothpaste was too strong, and the bristles felt weird in her mouth.

Remembering how Mrs. Sherriff had helped before, Molly decided to ask her for advice.

"Mrs. Sherriff, brushing my teeth doesn't feel good, and it's boring. The toothpaste tastes yucky, and the brush feels strange," Molly explained.

Mrs. Sherriff thought for a moment. "Let's try finding a toothpaste with a milder flavour, like strawberry or bubblegum.

We can also use a toothbrush with extra-soft bristles. And how about we make brushing fun by singing a special 'Toothbrush Song' while you brush?" Molly giggled. "That sounds fun!"

That evening, Molly's Mum helped her find a strawberry-flavored toothpaste and a soft-bristled toothbrush.

They sang the 'Toothbrush Song' together, making the routine enjoyable.

Despite these improvements, Molly still felt overwhelmed by her morning routine. She often forgot important steps of getting ready and felt rushed.

Noticing her struggle, Mrs. Sherriff suggested creating a visual checklist to help.

Together, they made a colorful checklist with pictures showing each step: waking up, brushing teeth, getting dressed, eating breakfast, and packing her school bag.

Molly decorated the checklist with her favourite stickers, making it special.

With her new colourful checklist, Molly's mornings became smoother and less frustrating.

She followed each step and even had extra time to play before school.

Mrs. Sherriff praised Molly's efforts. "You've done a wonderful job, Molly; I know sometimes things can be difficult. By finding solutions that work for you, you can make everyday tasks easier and more fun."

Molly beamed with pride, ready to tackle any tricky task that came her way.

Feeling proud, Molly shared her 'Helpful Check List' with her classmates, inspiring them to create their own.

Here is a copy of my helpful checklists; you can create your own to help and make them more colourful if you wish.

Molly's Check List
Morning

- ✓ Eat Breakfast
- ✓ Clothes On
- ✓ Brush Teeth
- ✓ Brush Hair
- ✓ Pack Bag
- ✓ Hug
- ✓ Smile

Molly's Check List
Evening

- ✓ Eat Dinner
- ✓ Spellings
- ✓ Read Book
- ✓ PJs On
- ✓ Brush Teeth
- ✓ Good Night

Acknowledgements

Thanks to all the support I have around me, including the Oasis Team at Jumeriah English Speaking School (JESS) and my favourite teacher in the whole world, Mrs Sherriff, who makes school easier for me.

www.ingramcontent.com/pod-product-compliance
Lightning Source LLC
Chambersburg PA
CBHW041439120626
46547CB00002B/269